LOOKING BACK AT
Ellesmere Port
Pat O'Brien

Willow
PUBLISHING

Willow Publishing
Willow Cottage, 36 Moss Lane,
Timperley, Altrincham,
Cheshire, WA15 6SZ

©Pat O'Brien 1986

ISBN 0 946361 18 5

Printed by The Commercial
Centre Ltd., Hollinwood, Oldham.

This book is dedicated to my wife Norah Rowens, who made it all possible.

Pat O'Brien was born in 1924, the youngest son of a distinguished soldier, Capt. D. O'Brien, D.C.M., M.S.M. He was educated in the C.B. St. Canice's School, and Bolton Street Technical College, Dublin. In 1942 he joined H.M. Forces and saw Active Service in Sicily, Italy, and Holland with the Parachute Regt. He was taken P.O.W. at Arnhem.

He has been researching local history since 1963, and since early retirement from Burmah Oil Ltd. in 1981, when they closed down their local refinery, he has been giving talks to schools and local organisations. This is his second book on the area.

He is a registered guide for the City of Chester with the North West Tourist Board. He also teaches local history at the Grange Adult Centre.

Introduction

This is not intended to be a history of the area, because I have already written one, "Our Local Heritage", (1980). It is a pictorial glimpse of places that have gone, or been altered considerably. The text is a collation of documented facts, and local people's reminiscences.

I wish to thank the following people for their help with information, and the loan of old postcards, photographs, etc. Mrs. M. Gillam, Chief Librarian Ellesmere Port Central Library, Mr. M. Crossland, Editor of the Ellesmere Port Pioneer, Mr. L. G. Lynch, Mr. R. Hignett, Mr. C. Parker, Mrs. Byrne, Mrs. Gould, Mrs. Lloyd, Mrs. N. Knight, Mrs. L. Smith, Mr. E. Percival, Mr. M. Day, Mr. McCrone, Mr. T. Speakman, Mr. Farrington. For photocopying my thanks to Mr. M. Day.

A debt of gratitude to Mrs. Beryl Newns, for interpreting my manuscripts of twelve years research, and typing them.

If I have forgotten anyone for their help, please accept my thanks.

P. A. O'Brien, 1986.

Gersham Stewart, MP for Wirral, visiting Eastham after the Election in 1910.

The Chester Canal

The Company's instructions in 1791 were: 'From the Chester Canal Basin the proposed Canal to proceed . . . locking up as high conveniently may be; so as to carry the Canal on a level through the Backford valley near Wervin to the River Mersey near Stanlow House and Poole Hall being a distance of ten miles' (ELC 1/4 15th September, 1791).

A clause in the Act, however, forced the canal to swing to the north side of Backford valley to avoid Moston Hall. On emerging at Stoke, the route was aimed directly at Ince; the surveyors were thus compelled to reroute their line immediately after leaving the Broxton valley, and provided an almost right-angled bend just east of Stoke. The canal was then carried as close as possible to the marshland edge to meet the Mersey not in Netherpool but in Whitby township.

The Company showed foresight in cutting the Wirral Line first, for not only was it relatively easy to construct but it was also the vital estuarial link, capable of supporting immediately a remunerative traffic between Chester and the Mersey and thus helping to finance more arduous construction in the hinterland. As early as 1791, all proposed trunk lines had specified that the Wirral Line should be built to take boats of 14ft beam, although the remainder of the canal was built solely on narrow gauge lines (ELC 1/4 15th September, 1791).

The exact date of completion is not known. An 'elegant passage boat' was launched into the canal at Chester on 8th June, 1795 (Chester Courant 12th June, 1795) but the passenger service was not begun until the 1st July (Gore's Liverpool General Advertiser 9th July, 1795). The three locks into the Mersey were not finished until early 1796. There is no record of a celebration; the initiation of goods traffic was quietly made by the familiar string of coal boats, which reached Chester from the Mersey in February 1796, (Nottingham Journal 27th February, 1796).

The broad Wirral line, specifically constructed to enable Mersey vessels to reach Chester, (Turner (1971) p.6) was less an attempt to revitalise the ancient port than to use its social capital as a basis for a transhipment

Rock breaking machines in the Poole Hall cutting

point between the broad and narrow sections of the Ellesmere Canal. But basic installations were also found to be necessary at the Mersey outfall in the area known as Stanley House. The terminal was designated 'Ellesmere Port' by the Company as early as 1795 (ELC 1/1 21st December, 1795).

The local inhabitants referred to the new settlement as Whitby Wharf or Whitby Locks. The local and regional names were used side-by-side as late as the 1860's when the railway station was named Whitby Locks, and the name persisted in the term 'Locks goods', used into the 20th Century on Liverpool docks.

The Initial Terminal

The canal entered Whitby township some distance from the hamlet, but only a half a dozen meadows were involved. In March 1795 a Company surveyor was ordered to value the land taken for the Wirral line but not yet paid for (ELC 1/1 6th March, 1795). Apparently the land at the terminus was not acquired until after the completion of the canal, for contemporary minute books reveal the proprietors' vexation at the high prices demanded by landowners. These were so high that the Company's agents were instructed to buy the smallest area possible, consistent

Filling in the tidal basin inside the lighthouse area.

with its plans, (ELC 1/2 10th February, 1797). Thus Ellesmere Port was founded on a very restricted site, parts of the vital Merseyside fields 113 – 15 being purchased from Earl Grosvenor. All told, the area on which the new port was built covered less than four acres. The purchased portions of both 114 and 115 were intended for docks. The descent to the Mersey, about 30 ft, was accomplished by means of three broad locks which reached a tidal basin via three small side basins.

The stillwater dock at summit level was constructed rather as an appendix to this scheme in both scope and shape, the latter conditioned by the restrictive boundaries of the estate. Excavation in the marl was not difficult, and the spoil was dumped along the canal sides. Water deficiencies were overcome by the erection of a 'fire engine', capable of transferring a 'lockful of water per hour' from the tidal to the upper dock, (ELC 1/2 26th September, 1796).

Open space remaining was used as wharfage, though a small warehouse was ordered to be built in 1795. In the minutes of 1796 appears an order 'that the Wirral Line . . . be extended from the Basin at Whitby on the summit level in a direct line to the further Basin made upon the level of the River Mersey', (ELC 1/2 23rd June, 1796). The disadvantages of the cul-de-sac nature of the upper dock had quickly been appreciated, but though improvements were later made, this direct water link was never constructed.

Telford had been made responsible for planning all 'Bridges, Aqueducts, Tunnels, Locks, Reservoirs, Buildings, Wharfs and other works' on the canal (ELC 1/1 23rd September, 1793). A recognised architect, his talents were given little scope at Ellesmere Port in the face of limited supplies of both land and money.

No building graced the site in 1795. The demands of passenger traffic, however, soon made imperative the construction of some form of accommodation at the terminal. Not wishing to extend its obligations, the Company asked Whitby landowners if they were willing to provide suitable buildings, warehouses and wharfs. The landowners were not interested; by September, Telford was seeking a contractor to carry out the construction of a public house and warehouse to the Company's plans, (ELC 1/1 7th May, 8th June, 9th

September, 1795).

In the following year the proprietors sought to erect dwellings for canal workers, but no such dwellings had appeared in Ellesmere Port by 1902. As most of the line's business was transacted at Chester, regular employees at the Port were few.

On the slope between the locks and the upper basin a small inn was built with two small dwellings and stables nearby. A lock-keeper's cottage commanded the junction of canal, locks and dock. The tavern was reported complete in 1801, and the ground around it cleared and levelled 'so as to be clean and commodious for travellers', (Telford's Report 25th November, 1801, quoted in Roberts p.24). A number of shooting butts and bathing huts appeared on the Mersey shore.

The Courant, 13th June, 1809

'S. Ackerley, Canal Tavern, Chester, respectfully informs his friends and the public that a **Boat Coach** will commence running between this city and Wrexham on Wednesday next about half past two in the afternoon and continue running every day as soon as the boat comes in. It will return every day from the Pigeon Inn, in Wrexham in time for the boat for Liverpool, etc. Fare to Chester inside 4/6d, outside 3s. and to Liverpool inside 6/6d, outside4/6d.'

Sunday Canal Traffic

The barges frequently collected in the canal basin at Christleton particularly on a Sunday as they were not allowed to pass through Chester before 6 o'clock in the evening.

Here is an extract from –
"A Home Tour through the Manufacturing Districts of England in the Summer of 1835", by Sir G. Head

I made one voyage by this canal, from Chester towards Liverpool, by the packet-boat, which started from the canal basin at eleven o'clock in the morning. Notwithstanding the bad navigation of the River Dee necessarily tends to increase the traffic on this canal.

THE DOCKS. ELLESMERE PORT.

The Iron Raddle Wharf.

Industries of all kinds were now arriving on the banks of the Mersey. Works were built at Widnes and Runcorn. When these works were established on the eastern banks of the Mersey a curious thing happened. The banks began to move from the eastern to the western side, with the consequence that the water left our shores and only mud and sand was left between tides. This silting up of the river bank caused considerable disorganization and expense to the Company, as when the tide was low the steamers that towed the flats, "Lord Clive" and the "Earl of Powis", could not get up to the docks and men had to haul the flats up to the wharfs from the steamer and back to the steamer from the wharfs. When the tides were low it

was not possible to load flats 3′ or 3′6″, and gangs of men had to go and discharge the flats into others to the required draught. These gangs worked five men to a gang and worked piecework, everything having to be manhandled. Only men of robust physique were capable of standing the strain. The men were paid by the ton, and so expert were they at this class of work that with mechanical regularity they could handle many tons per hour without the least signs of exhaustion.

In 1860 the London and North Western Railway Company took over the control of the Shropshire Union Canal Company, and trade continued to be very brisk. Ton upon ton of furnace iron was conveyed down the canal from Wolverhampton. Load upon load

of fire-bricks and fire-clay were brought down from the Potteries bound for America. Boats were going night and day, and there was plenty of work to spare for everyone. Later however, this trade died down never to return.

The Flats and the Grain Trade

The flats were extremely strongly built and were unable to carry more than thirty or forty tons on a draught of 4ft which was the limit allowed on the canal. The captain of a flat received 12s. per week, and the mate 8s. Those were the wages they received if they did not do a stroke of work. They were also paid tonnage or commission on every ton carried on the flat. Ton money amounted to 3d. per ton from Ellesmere Port to Liverpool, and vice-versa. From Liverpool to Chester the rate went up to 9d. per ton, the reason being that the journey from Ellesmere Port to Chester was a slow one; being hauled by a horse it took eight hours.

Flatmen and porters employed by the Shropshire Union were only paid once a fortnight, on a Friday. It was a standing custom that the wives or mothers of the employees drew the wages, and one might see a long row of women going down to the office to draw the wages, all dressed in shawls and white aprons. The men called it white apron day. All transactions between local shopkeepers was done on the credit system, which was necessary owing to the fortnightly pay days.

The first thing that a flatman's wife would do after receiving her husband's wages, would be to go and pay her bill at the grocer's, baker's or butcher's. They all carried a credit or 'tommy' book, and sometimes owing to a slack week or two, some of the less thrifty fell into arrears. To meet these arrears, it was the practice to keep two pigs which they fed and sold to the butchers, one of the pigs was looked upon as set aside for the shopkeeper, and the other for themselves to buy boots and clothing and other items for the house.

Before transferring their business to Ellesmere Port, Messrs. Frost & Sons Flour Mill was established at Chester, and the wheat was conveyed from Liverpool to Ellesmere Port in flats, and then on to Chester by canal. In those days before grain elevators, all the grain had to be bushelled by two men and it was the duty of the flatmen to hold the sacks into which the grain was emptied. The bags were then tied, two at a time, by nippers and hoisted into the mill. The foreman at the mill was a man named John Smith, who resided at Steam Mill Street, Chester. When the flats were drawing up to the mill wharf, he would be waiting with a bread tin for the flatmen to get him a sample of the grain. John Smith was a kind old fellow, but very asthmatical which he thought a drop of gin would cure, and the young flatmen who desired to remain in Chester for the weekend, and whose flat was likely to finish discharging before Saturday evening, found that by interviewing John and taking him to the "Cross Foxes" for a drop of gin, the matter was satisfactorily arranged.

The Whaling Story

Before the M.S.C. was built an unusual happening took place. The Packet boat was bringing a loaded tow of barges from Liverpool when four very large fish were observed on the top of the water, following in the boats wake. The fish proved to be a small shoal of whales that had got into the river. One of the shoal was stranded on the Shropshire Union slipway and another was found in one of the river locks. When it was found that the whale on the slipway was fast, a local butcher named Platt was sent for, and he arrived with his knives. Mr. Platt found it a rather difficult job to dispatch the whale, which was ultimately fastened to the Packet boat and towed back to Liverpool where it was sold to an oil merchant. The second one found its way into one of the river locks which took the float from the river basin to the small canal. It appears that a flat was being in the process of being lowered from the small canal to the river level. The lock gateman, fearing that an obstruction of some kind was stopping the lock from functioning properly, pushed a boathook down the side of the barge into the lock, when an obstruction, that under the boathook felt for all the world like a lump of indiarubber, was found. Suspecting that something out of the ordinary was happening, the water was returned to the lock, and the flat taken out, and up came the whale, spouting about thirty feet high. It was a great sight, and one that was talked about for years. The whale was taken into the canal basin, loaded into a canal boat, and shipped to Wolverhampton, where it was exhibited.

Ellesmere Port Docks.

Warehouses and hydraulic cranes

The Hydraulics

The top hydraulic was situated behind the Island Warehouse and operated the cranes in the top area, the jiggers (hoists inside the warehouses) capstans, buzzers, and also pumped down water to the mills for washing down grains.

The bottom hydraulic, opposite the lighthouse, supplied power to four cranes on the North Wall, to various capstans, also the coal tip and the Clay warehouses.

Situated about were several towers used in the Hydraulic system, each containing a water tank with counterbalanced weights and called accumulators. Work would cease if the water level in the accumulators was low, or the cranes or capstans leaked pressure.

On the coal tips the hydraulic lifts would elevate coal wagons (20 tons) and tip them. This coal was for use on M.S.C. boats. Other special coal was brought up to the Basin Gas Works, in three wagons on a float, which were unloaded into wheelbarrows. It would take four men six hours to unload.

The Top Hydraulic was kept working continuously in case of fire etc. The Bottom Hydraulic only operated in the day time.

Extracts from the Lancashire Merchants and Ship Canal News

Section 1

'This section continues to make very rapid progress. The cutting at Netherpool has been stripped of its coating of clay. The steam crane has taken the place of the steam navvy, which has now to seek soil more suitable for mastication by its gigantic teeth, than the hard rock that has been laid bare. The loud reports of frequent blasting takes the place of the chatter and rattle of the navvy chain. Long gullets have been cut from one end of the cutting to the other, which greatly facilitates the getting of the rock. Some of the rock is being dressed to form a face to the estuary embankments, and that which is not large enough for this purpose is taken to make the road by which the embankments are to be made.'

June 9th

Section 1

'There are now seven steam navvies working in the lock pits at Eastham, two are working in the second lift down, one of which has cut a gullet about 500 yards long and to a depth of 35 feet from the surface, the gullet is 50 feet wide and in very hard clay.

Two very large Lancashire boilers have been brought to supply steam for the large Cornish pumps that are to be put into the main sump, as it is expected much water will be met in the third lift, which will be in rock, and form an excellent foundation for the large locks to be built here. Much progress has been made with the estuary embankments, and the stone-dressing yard is assuming a very busy aspect, piles of stone being got ready for protecting the embankment. This section is now connected with Section No.2 by telephone.'

June 16th

'New ground has been opened out here this week near Boston Wood and a steam navvy started in the cutting. This will connect the work making one continuous line from Eastham to Ellesmere Port. This week, rock has been struck in the cutting at a depth of 35 feet; another lift of about 15 feet has to come out, which will be all rock. This would naturally be supposed to be against the work, but really it will be a great saving to the contractor, who can utilise the stone thus got on the spot, in the building of walls and embankments. The brickyard here is now complete and the kilns burning. A large amount of good brick earth is found here which will be sufficient for all bricks needed.

The embankment here across the bed of the river will be over one mile in length, and the top width 20 feet, with a slope of 1 in 1. Pool Hall Brook has given some trouble as it is too low to run into the Canal. A culvert has had to be cut 60 feet deep to carry the waters of the brook under the Canal; the cutting on the Ellesmere side of the brook is, with the exception of about 10 feet on the top, all rocks, and the contractor estimates that in this cutting alone, there are over half a million tons of rock to be excavated.

The hospital at Ellesmere Port, which is provided by Mr. Walker for the use of the Eastham and Ince

sections, is now opened. The hospital is constructed to hold twenty beds in the men's ward and eight beds in the ward for women and children.

At Eastham there are 72 huts for living quarters, each hut large enough for a family and some eight to twelve lodgers in addition. At Netherpool an ancient pathway has been found running in a south-easterly direction at a depth of 15 feet below the surface, and on top of this soil are trees growing up to 30 feet diameter.

It consists of 4, 5, and 6 inch boulders edged with rough hewn ashlers, 6 inches thick, and about 10 to 12 inches deep, varying in length. The stones are imbedded on a bank of clay of about 12 to 18 inches deep, this would seem to indicate that it was thus raised up by the side of the stream as it lies on the old Sias clay, and the debris caused by the overflow of the stream.'

Pile driving on the foreshore of Ellesmere Port.

The latter stages in the excavation near Ellesmere Port.

Section 2

'Before the construction of the Helsby to Hooton railway line Ince Pier was a very busy spot, as all communication between this neighbourhood and distant places was made by river, the pier being used for passengers, and also for goods of all descriptions. At that time the house on the right of the pier was a fully-licensed public house, and some idea may be had of the traffic, because the landlord, besides paying what was then thought a heavy rent, cleared £69 week. After the railway was made, traffic to the pier gradually decreased, and the license was allowed to lapse. The construction of the Canal has again given a busy appearance to the place.

A temporary bridge has been built over the River Gowy. Coals and heavy material for the Ellesmere Port side of this section are brought and owing to some dispute with the River Commissioners, the contractor has not been allowed to make a temporary wharf, but has to bring a steam crane on the bridge, and wind all the materials out of the boats into the waggons which are brought alongside the crane.'

July 19th 1898

'Miss Simpson has been appointed head nurse at the Ellesmere Port Hospital, and great interest is taken in it by the gentry in the neighbourhood who kindly supply pictorial and other interesting publications for the use of the patients. The grounds in front of the hospital are being laid out, and every care is being taken that the poor fellows who have the misfortune to become inmates have every attention and comfort.

In No. 1 Section, work is now carried on night and day. Three steam navvies are kept continually at work from the break of day on Monday, until darkness sets in on Saturday. The number of men has been increased by over 100, bringing up the total on this section alone to nearly 900. Another steam navvy has been erected and got to work this week, and one more locomotive, making a total of eight steam navvies and fourteen locomotives. Great interest is taken in the works by Liverpudlians who come every day in large numbers by railway and steamboat to inspect the works. That part of Eastham bordering on the river has greatly altered in appearance, the contractor's yard here, which five months ago was a green field, is now crossed by six lines of rails and looks very much like a large railway goods station. The total length of rails in this section is upwards of fourteen miles. A connection has now been made with this section and the railway at Ellesmere Port Station, so that the tracks can be brought from the railway right on the works. A line of rails has also been laid connecting the works with the Shropshire Union Railway and Canal Co's. docks at Ellesmere Port. The injuries to the fitter named Gamble, who was knocked down by a locomotive on this section last week, are of a more serious nature than was first thought. On examination at Birkenhead Hospital, it was found that in addition to his feet being badly crushed, three of his ribs were broken, his arm fractured, his shoulder dislocated, and his head severely cut.'

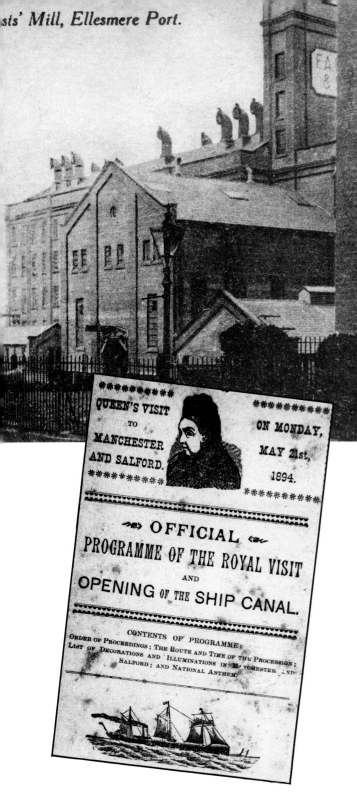

sts' Mill, Ellesmere Port.

Flour Mills, Ellesmere Port.

The Flour Mills

The first flour mill in Ellesmere Port was the Imperial Flour Mills. Their lease from 1st OCTOBER, 1904, was for a term of 99 years at an annual rental of £200 to the Shropshire Union, who for their part were to construct a dock arm or waterway, wharf and a railway siding to serve the mill. The mill was the first in the country to be fitted with a plansifter mill.

It was followed in 1906 by the King Flour Mills. The third mill, F. A. Frost and Sons, came from Chester, and commenced operations in September, 1910.

In 1921 the mills, Imperial, King's and Frost's employed respectively 50, 30 and 60 men.

The Imperial closed down in 1929, later reopening in 1930 and now operating for Joseph Rank. Still later it was reconditioned, and restarted in July, 1940. Imperial finally closed down in 1955; Frost's in 1957. King's lasted longer, but it too closed in the 1960s.

The first illustration shows Frost's Mill in 1919. In the 1930s they had six steam traction for delivery purposes, and it was the job of a Mr. Hubert Mayers to go in at 3.45a.m. and start up the fires in the traction engines, so that they would be on steam by the time the drivers came in at 6.30a.m.

The second illustration shows the "Canal Arm" behind the mills. Alongside the mills can be seen the big barges offloading their cargo of grain into the mills. The grain was brought from abroad by ship to Liverpool or Birkenhead Docks, here transhipped to barges and brought along the M.S.C. to the mills. The 20 ton narrow boats on the right took the finished flour in 140lb. sacks to Birmingham.

The Cement Works

The Stanlow Works Estate Ltd. (later renamed The Ship Canal Portland Cement Manufacturers Ltd.) was registered on the 31st January, 1911. It changed hands many times, and because of a savage price war in the 1920s, the business went from bad to worse, until the end finally came in 1932 with a loss of 400 jobs.

The Oil Industry

The M.S.C. began construction of an oil dock at Stanlow in 1916, and it was completed in June, 1922. Shell–Mex came here in 1923, starting on a 27 acre site. It started as a small tankage installation handling and redistributing refined petroleum products. Later in 1924 it developed a small bitumen processing plant. Today it is one of the largest refineries in the country.

THE PONTOON DRY DOCK, ELLESMERE PORT.   R.G.D.

Ship Building

The Pontoon Dock, capable of dealing with vessels of up to 5,500 tons burden was moored in its excavated berth at Ellesmere Port in October, 1893. It was a Tyneside concern, but an agreement was made with the Manchester Ship Canal Co. that vessels entering the Ship Canal for repairs only were to be exempt from canal dues if the work was carried out by the Dry Docks Co., while vessels could lie free-of-charge in the Company's own private wharfs whilst undergoing repairs.

Dock Workers' Reminiscences

In 1908, fenders made out of hemp ropes 70' long 6' × 6', in the workshops, were pulled by one horse. There were change horses at Chester Tower Wharf and stables at Bunbury, Hack Green, Market Drayton and Autherley. This was a journey of about 3 hours. Goods would be pulled into Telfords Warehouse, checked and transferred into the narrow boats in the Cross Berth (where the crane is).

The Island Warehouse mostly stocked bag stuff and the Crate Warehouse (next to the bottom lock) stored goods for transhipping. Family boats would have a two cabin boat, one fore and aft. A Nurse Blain and Tom Shone would cater for first aid needs. Nurse Blain used Porters Row as a medical room. The last building in Porters Row was called the Galley where the men used to dine; at the back and alongside was the fire engine shed. A church service would be held for the boat people in the Central Hall. The present canteen was the old Mission Hall, Mr. Baddiley was the preacher and they gave a party at Christmas. Mr. James Atherton of the Boat House had trotting horses. At the rear entrance to the Island Warehouse was the Indecking Dock where the boats were tested for what they would carry, and for leakages.

Weights would be lowered by crane into the boats, and would be checked against the three copper plates fixed on either side of the boats, one forward, one middle and one aft. The plates would have lines on approx. 1 ton to the inch. Thus the load could be gauged looking at the depth of the line.

The iron one wharf was called the Raddle Wharf. The tugs from Chester to Ellesmere Port and vice-versa were 5.00a.m., 11.00a.m. and 3.00p.m. The horse could be left at Chester to await its owners return. If a boat owner had a good horse he would keep it for his own use. The big slipway was for the bigger barges and tugs to repair them. 'Lord Stalybridge' and 'W. E. Dorrington' were the tugs between Ellesmere Port and Liverpool. The tugs to Chester were 'The Luna', 'The Dagmar' and the 'Rocket' (J. Challinor).

Cecil Parker started work in September, 1914 at the age of 14 in the Grain Warehouse sorting out sacks for

The Ship Canal and Grain Elevator, Ellesmere Port.

use. Two men or three lads were employed trimming down the grain and putting it down the chute, to be bagged up. Because of the war, women were employed in various jobs. Basic hours were 56½ per week. Basic wages were 12/- a week. Work started at 6.00a.m. till ½ hour breakfast at 8.00a.m. Dinner was 12 till 1.00p.m. A break for tea was between 5.30 and 6.00p.m. Work then continued till 9.00p.m. £1 could be earned with overtime. Monday to Friday. Saturday working hours were 2.00 to 5.00p.m. Each worker had a metal tally with his work number on it.

2nd September, 1922 started M.S.C. took over May 1st, worked bunkering up ships on M.S.C. near the nitre sheds that held explosives, brought up by sailing boats or barges. The nitre was brought in sailing ships from S. America and unloaded at the Old Quay. It was loose, like a dirty salt, always transported in hessian sacks, to await transhipping by rail.

Before the Great War, sailing ships with a large door 50ft. each side of the bow, would fetch telegraph poles from Scandinavia. The first lot of poles were pulled out into the water and a raft formed which would be later broken up when the rest had been unloaded and hydraulic capstan used. The China Clay ships came from Cornwall; they were sailing ships, unloaded by hydraulic cranes into tubs on the first floor on rails, which would take the clay in and tip it down to the ground floor. The narrow boats would be loaded up from the ground floor by wheelbarrow.

Dock Street

Houses were first built here in the 1840s, and changed into shops in the 1850s. At this time the Postmaster, Mr. James Cox lived here, there were two grocers and three public houses, the Grosvenor Arms, the Bulls Head, and the Dock Hotel. The view shows it in 1905. The shops were as follows: Liversley, provisions; Mounsey, outfitters; Cottrels, fruit and vegetables; Hughes, fish; Tomlin, shoe repairs; Wallbank, newsagent; Turner, butcher; Salter, newsagent; Summers, millinery; Stocktons, grocery; Finlay, tailor; Jefferson, shoe repairs; Drummond, chemist; Meredith, fruit; Breeze, fish and chips; Hughes, bakery; Stockton, butcher. All these shops have been demolished.

The Police Sergeant is believed to be a Sgt. Bellhouse.

Victoria Park was a small rectangular park bounded by Queen Street, Upper Mersey Street, and Dock Street. At small eastern end were the backs of properties in Queen Street and Dock Street. Up till the 1930s it was the principal park in the town. On Sunday evenings in the summertime there would be band concerts. An excerpt from the local paper: '10th May, 1925. Last Sunday after a dull morning, the weather picked up and became a lovely evening, and both inside and outside the railings of Victoria Park a crowd estimated to be a 1,000 people stood and listened to the music of the Public Prize Band. Mr. Arthur Price excelled in playing solo on the euphonium "The Old Folks at Home".'

The park is now sadly gone.

The view of "The Grosvenor" shows it decorated for the Coronation of George V in 1911. It is still there on its own below the motorway.

Mr. Brekon's School, and The Institute

In 1872 the Methodists built their Central Hall in Upper Mersey Street to be used for both religious and educational activities. The first schoolmaster was a Mr. W. Brekon. An account of his arrival by an old "Portite" makes interesting reading.

'The village was let into the secret of his coming, and had been looking forward to his coming with a keen anticipation which can only be found in very small towns like Ellesmere Port was in those days. The whole village turned out to have a look at him. And how disappointed everyone felt when a mild-looking young gentleman came down the road. We had conjured in our minds a stately stern man, wearing fierce side whiskers and a withering eye. "Why, he is only a boy, but he has a pleasant face. He will have to be careful or the boys will be turning on him", it was said.'

The new schoolmaster soon took an active interest in his new home town and at one period had a drum and fife band under his command. It would tour round the villages collecting funds for the "Prims" Sunday School outings to Frodsham Hills. It is said that he composed a tune called "The Ellesmere Port Grand March". He also served on the local council.

The Institute was also built by the "Prims" in 1888, in Queen Street, and even had a billiard room. It was used for various functions but never became a financial success. It was taken over by the Government in 1912 as a Labour Exchange, and was demolished to form part of the new motorway.

The view of Queens Street (formerly Poole Street) shows the Central Hall at the far end in Upper Mersey Street.

Station Road

This road was originally a cart track leading from
Whitby to the Mersey shore and Netherpoole. In the
1860s the carrying trade was flourishing in Ellesmere
Port; the Whitby farmers found that sending their
produce to Liverpool via the Shropshire Union Canal
was much cheaper and quicker than taking it by cart,
via the Riveracre Valley Road. They decided to make
the lane down to the shore into a road, which was done
using gravel from the river shore, and thus built what
might be termed the first real connection with the
outside world.

When the railway opened up in 1863, between
Hooton and Helsby it was built across this road and a
station built there, thus the name Station Road. The
view is of the Railway Hotel on 5th January, 1905. It
was then known as Mc. Garva's Railway Hotel. It was
extended on the right-hand side in 1909, and the hotel
was re-named the Station Hotel. In 1912, the left-hand
side was extended and was said to have the longest bar
in Cheshire. A story is told about the old "Railway
Hotel", that the foreman platelayer missed some of his
men, so he went to the "Railway Hotel" and found
them there, but they had a good answer. They said they
were shifting the 'points'.

On the right-hand side of the level crossing can be
seen the slope leading down to the "Cattle Arch". This
was a tunnel leading under the railway lines for
livestock and pedestrians who did not wish to be
delayed by trains. It is now buried under the
Westminster Bridge.

The Parish Churches

The first Parish Church, opened for divine service in 1842, was a pretty little edifice, built of stone and having lattice windows all round. It was fitted with old fashioned pews, which had high doors at each end, the accommodation for school children being rough deal benches in the middle. It had room for 270 people. The only music provided for conducting the services was a tuning fork.

Each Ash Wednesday all the porters employed by the Shropshire Union Canal Company had to attend the Parish Church when the bell rang at ten o'clock in the morning. They went straight from their work, just in their rough and soil stained clothes. The service usually took the form of prayers and a short sermon. This church was situated further over in the graveyard, (see the 1871 plan) facing onto Church Street.

Christ Church shown in the view, was the second Parish Church. With donations raised from the Canal Company and the Duke of Westminster, this much larger church was constructed on Station Road. It cost £2,900 to build, and was opened in 1869. In 1871 a new Ecclesiastical Parish of Ellesmere Port was formed and the new church was consecrated with a special Confirmation Service.

The parsonage was built in 1852–3 with a contribution from the Canal Company. It was demolished when a new Vicarage was built in Whitby, in conjunction with the new church of St. Thomas built in 1960.

Early Entertainment

In December of 1908 a hall, called the Church Institute, was built at the end of Grosvenor Street by local church people to replace a mission hall that had been destroyed by fire the previous year, and had stood at the corner of Queen Street. Here were held dances, socials and meetings. In its first year, a new maple floor was laid to cater for the newest craze that was sweeping the country – roller skating. The charge for admission was sixpence, including skates. Magic lantern shows were also held there, to be followed by a new marvel of the age – moving pictures.

By 1910 a larger theatre was needed to cater for the growing community and so a new one was built in Meadow Lane. The Church Institute was turned into a dance hall. Although only a corrugated iron structure, the new Hippodrome was a great attraction. It staged melodramas and variety acts, from "The Murder of Maria Martin", to the local "Keystone Kops". On Saturday nights people would queue for hours to get in, and the gaily-clad "boat people" who commandeered the balconies that ran along the sides of the theatre, would keep the rest of the audience amused with their language and antics. They always seemed to be supplied with monkey nuts, with the shells of which they pelted the more "select" section of the audience seated below in the stalls. When a new cinema, the "Queens" was built in 1913, the Hippodrome gave up its live shows in favour of the "movies". About 1928 a new and magnificent Hippodrome cinema was built in Carnegie Street. Today the Church Institute is gone, "The Queens" is a bingo hall, the old Hippodrome a somewhat changed social club, and the new Hippodrome a car showroom.

The First Post Office

The first Post Office was in Dock Street, and was kept by a Mr. James Cox. No letters were delivered from the post office, but were brought from Chester by a postman whose name was Jack Hall. From Chester he travelled through Stoak and Stanney delivering his letters, until he arrived at Ellesmere Port, where he would complete his delivery. The postman stayed at the Canal Tavern all day, and in the evening would gather up his letters and return to Chester by road.

The official times stated in a directory of 1869 are as follows: 'Letters from all parts arrive (from Chester) at seven morning, and are despatched thereto at ten minuits past six evening.'

Whitby Road, Cambridge Road School

It was built in 1909, by the County Council, the first of its kind in Ellesmere Port. Until that time schools had been administered by the churches and chapels. It was the latest in modern design with large playgrounds, and was co-educational apart from woodwork classes for the boys, and laundry and housewifery for girls.

Ellesmere Port Railway Station

In Slaters Directory of Cheshire of 1869, the name given to the railway station was Whitby (one-third of a mile from Ellesmere Port); John Evans was the Station Master.

The local paper "Ellesmere Port Pioneer" had this to say in the 1920s on railway matters. "We wish to refrain from publishing the select language which one hears from workmen going to work, and having to lose a half-hours pay because a goods train is allowed to shunt in the station.

"Why do Ellesmere Port passengers receive open air treatment, whilst Little Sutton has the luxury of an enclosed room on the "Up" platform? The "Helsby" girls have to be at the Station at 6.20a.m. on Monday morning's if they want their weeklies."

The Level Crossing was replaced by the Westminster Bridge on the 20th July, 1961, and opened by the Rt. Hon. Selwyn Lloyd. The famous "Cattle Arch" was filled in.

Whitby Road

The houses on the left-hand side of Whitby Road, were called Stanlow Cottages. They were built in 1899 for the benefit of workers at the local Smelting Works. It was situated where Octel is today. In 1906 seven shops were built on the opposite side to Stanlow Cottages, the first one being occupied by a Mr. H. W. Wallis, a chemist who later acquired the adjoining premises as a Sub Post Office. The shop can be seen on the corner of Cambridge Road, opposite Caswells Pawn Shop. The pledge office was in Cambridge Road at the rear of the main shop. Mr. Caswell came to Ellesmere Port about 1910, and lived above his other shop on the corner of Exeter Road, where drapery and baby wear were sold. The next view shows that the buildings on the same side were extended as far as Exeter Road, but nothing beyond this. This view is wrongly titled Station Road. The third view shows the corner of Exeter Road with the same corner roof sticking out, and also showing Meredith's fruit and vegetable shop, with their delivery cart outside.

On the corner of both Whitby and Exeter Roads can be seen a once famous local grocers called Dysons. In 1937 they moved into Exeter Road, when the whole corner was taken over by the firm of Montague Burton Ltd., and the frontage was completely restyled. It still stands out from all the other buildings in the original block. The rest of the buildings have remained the same basic structure from the first floor level to the roof; only the street level fronts have been altered from time to time to suit a particular product.

Whitby Road

The next view of Whitby Road further up shows the "Knot Hotel", Salter's newsagent, and J. S. Cartwright's shops. In later years to become the first "Woolworth's". The view of the "Knot" (this card is always misspelt) shows shop premises on the corner of Victoria Road. The "Knot" opened in 1910, and is reputed to get its name from the Staffordshire knot, from where many local families originated.

Further up the road, in 1911 the Co-op Society extended their premises by building a hall above their shop. Thus the "Co-op Hall" came into being. It was a popular venue for dances, and all kinds of shows. The Co-op corner to the corner of Stanney Lane was fenced off with iron railings, but gaps would appear here and there and children would take over natural possession.

In those days the Co-op had horses for their delivery carts, bread, milk and coal. Because they used to put their horses out to graze on these fields, they became known as the "Co-op field". Needless to say the horses were borrowed for the odd gallop by the more adventuresome.

There was a paddling pool on this field, when it became a general recreation ground, in the charge of a Mr. B. Clay. Today it is the Civic Centre and Bus Station area.

Whitby Road (Stanney Lane Corner)

In the view shown where the building is behind the trees, was once the site of A. F. Norman's Iron Foundry, where products such as grids and manhole covers were made. The house alongside was occupied by Mr. Norman senior, and later by his son Alec. Later on, the house was occupied by Mr. C. Stockton, the local butcher. Much later still, the yard and house were taken over by Perkin's the builders.

The site is now occupied by the block of the Borough Council offices.

Rose Cottage

The last occupants were Mr and Mrs Ellis Percival. Ellis had eight brothers and six sisters and worked for a while on the Manchester Ship Canal. One of his brothers, Charles, was a skipper of a dumb barge called Bactia which carried steel from Burnell's Ironworks to Liverpool and brought back grain from the flour mills. Four to six dumb barges were towed, at a time, by a steam tug.

The School in Stanney Lane

In between the thatched cottage and the house opposite was a very much smaller Stanney Lane than there is today.

On the left-hand side going down from this corner, just beyond the house, stood the school shown above, which was built over eighty years ago as a Church of England School. To everyone who went there it was known as Miss Gerrard's School.

Behind the railings on the left-hand side of the playground can be seen an upright stone, the boundary stone of the parishes of Stoak and Eastham. The thatched cottage, other corner house and school, were demolished in 1958 to widen the road. The site of the thatched cottage is now occupied by the new and imposing Police Station, which was opened by the Duke of Edinburgh.

Whitby Village

The original name for the village inn, was the "Dog and Partridge", but this was later changed to the 'Sportsmans Arms'. To the locals however it will always be known as "Bondy's", after one of the owners. The first view shows it in the early 1900s, the second in the 1930s much altered. Today it bears no resemblence to either view, as over twenty years ago the complete building, both inside and out, was completely re-structured whilst business proceeded as usual.

Whitby Post Office was a combination of a bakehouse and a Post Office. It was once occupied by a Mr. Green, and from 1911 by a Mr. W. H. Backhouse. Later still by a Mr. & Mrs. Mellor who just ran the bakehouse. The Post Office returned here many years later, the side of the building in Vale Road was made into two shops, and after having had different tenants, the Post Office returned to its previous site for a further few years. In the cottage opposite, behind the tree, lived the Jenkins family. On Friday nights Mr. C. Jenkins used to make "Light Cakes", then have them delivered in baskets to the local shops. When gas was piped to the village, the lamp-post was used as a meeting place by the villagers for any special occasion.

Whitby Village

The first view shows the start of Chester Road, between Vale Road and Tom Price's shop. Beyond the shop was a small shed that was used by the Liberal candidate, a Mr. R. S. Dodd, for committee meetings, etc.

Whitby Village

The second view shows the start of Pooltown Road with the lamp-post in the centre, the base of which is surrounded by a kerb to protect it from the wheels of horse-drawn vehicles. The shop on the right-hand side was the village store, belonging to Tom Price; on the left-hand side was the blacksmiths shop; the smith was called Mr. Parsonage. In the same yard was a building belonging to Walton's the local undertaker, where the hearse was kept and coffins made. At times there were two other blacksmith's shops in Whitby, one was in what is now Thomas's yard, the other one was near the bottom of Vale Road on the right-hand side, where the little lane winds off behind the houses up on the bank. This blacksmith was called Mr. Jones, and he bought a piece of land off the Grace family, to construct this lane as an entrance to his blacksmith's shop.

Pooltown Villas were built about the turn of the century, because they were of a design completely different from the terraced houses that were springing up in the rest of the town, and they were nicknamed "Garden City". Over the past thirty years the meadows have been transformed into a very large council estate.

Chester Road

Chester Road started from Whitby Post Office. The Chester Road view looks back towards Pooltown Road corner. The last house on the right of the picture is the only house still intact and still with its garden in splendid isolation on the wide pavement. All the rest have been converted into shops; on the left-hand side stands Offley's Bro's garage.

The other picture shows houses on the opposite side being converted into shops in the 1930s. On the left of the picture stands John Lloyd (Squire of Whitby), a scrap metal dealer in the 1914–18 War. He owned most of Whitby, and lived in Orchard Farm alongside the Sportsmans Arms. This site now occupied by the Salvation Army Citadel.

Chester Road, Whitby

WHITBY HALL WHITBY

Whitby Hall and Whitby Fête

Whitby Hall shown above, was the second building to bear this name. The other one was known as the Old Hall, and was situated between the Stanney Lane end of Vale Road and Old Hall Drive, where the block of two pairs of semi-detached houses stand. When the new hall was built about 1860, the senior part of the Grace family moved there. Both halls were in the Parish of Stoak. In 1903 it was decided to organize a fête in the grounds and it was so successful that it became an annual event. The fête held in 1930 was on Saturday, September 6th. Admission was 6 pence for adults, or 4 pence if paid before the 4th of September. Children 2 pence. There were competitions of all sorts, sports, flower show, a baby show, jazz competition, prizes for fancy dress and decorated floats. The prizes were usually a £1 First Prize, 10/- Second Prize. Each driver of a horse-drawn lorry received a gift of five shillings.

The procession would form up at Cambridge Road

School and proceed to Whitby Hall via Wellington Road, York Road, Whitby Road to the Sportsmans Arms, turn into Vale Road into Stanney Lane and then to Whitby Hall. In the fancy dress section, a very popular local group was known as "Danny's Weirs" chain gang. They were a group of men dressed up as convicts, joined by lengths of chain and a black football. They won many prizes in this event. In the decorated float section, local tradesmen would go to great trouble to outshine their rivals. The firm of Percival & Catteralls, coal merchants, had a special set of harness for shows and fête days. They also used their best horse who was named "Kit".

Sadly on the following month, on October 10th, Miss Susannah Egerton Grace, only daughter of John Grace senior, died at Whitby Old Hall aged 10. Her brother John was the last of the family, Member of Parliament for Wirral from 1924–31. In 1931 the Local Council purchased Whitby Hall, and grounds.

Football

Organised football in Ellesmere Port started in 1892 when the team that had been playing only friendly games was entered in the Wirral league, which the following year changed its name to the West Cheshire Football League.

Playing on the Boathouse field they had many successes, including the winning of the Pyke Cup in 1904. The World War of 1914–18 curtailed its activities, and it had to wait until 1919 before being reformed. It then moved from the Boathouse field to a new home in Grace Road. In 1923 it moved again to York Road Stadium.

The season of 1921–22 produced a 'wonder team', they won the West Cheshire League Championship, the Pyke Cup, and the Wirral Senior Cup. Over the years many of the local players achieved national and international status. The roll of honour in the football world is endless, Sam Chedgzoy, famous as Everton and England's outside-right, Joe Mercer, Liverpool F.C., Arsenal etc., Stanley Cullis and not forgetting Dave Hickson. The Club were Cheshire League Champions, 1957–58, 1958–59 and 1959–60. Nowadays the venue is Thornton Road Stadium, and the local team is Ellesmere Port & Neston F.C.

The Wednesday League and the Works Teams

There was keen competition amongst the various works teams. Sam Chedgzoy mentioned already, was snapped up by Everton in 1910 for a transfer fee of £10 whilst playing for Burnells F.C. They first played on the field now known as the Railway Goods Yard, before moving to the Boathouse field. They were called the old "Sunflowers" (an emblem of the old Burnells Ironworks which the footballers wore on their shirts).

The Cement works was another team that achieved fame, and with help of several of that wonder Port team of 1921, they were admitted to the Cheshire County League in the 1921–22 season. The Wednesday League were grocers who only played on Wednesdays, because that was their half-day. The new local paper had a query in its issue of February 27th. "Who has possession of the Wednesday Cup?"

Primitive Methodism in Whitby

In the picture of Vale Road, the second building with the large bay window was known as "Highbury". In the years before the Methodist Chapel on the hill was built, the owner James Worrall loaned a room of his house for a conference of the Methodists, whose cause he strongly supported. The room in fact is the one with the bay window.

The Methodist Chapel was built in 1873. The view shows it in 1908. A feature of any local community, religious or otherwise, was its social occasions. The second picture shows a Primitive Methodist trip in 1907, from the Whitby Chapel. The second waggon has a headboard with the name Smeatham Market Gardener, Whitby. The Methodist trips nearly always used to go to Raby Mere, and have a picnic there.

The Chapel alas has sadly gone, to be replaced by a new one in another area, and on the old site, houses have been built.

Poole Hall and the Poole family

Of the three local families of aristocratic origin the Pooles were the oldest, being of least Anglo-saxon stock. Their history is long and varied, and worth reading in its entirety. The male line of the family came to an end with the death of Rev. Sir Henry Poole in 1821. His only son met his death when a boy of eleven at Westminster School, "choking on an orange pip".

The female line however has carried on, and the present direct descendent is a Brigadier Blencoe-Tillard, whose father Brigadier J. A. S. Blencoe-Tillard, sent me the photograph of "Waxy" who won the Derby for Sir Francis Poole, and the Derby Cup.

Poole Hall was in its day reputed to be one of the finest specimens of Tudor architecture existing in the county. It was built or re-built about 1540, and extended in 1574 as appears from a date over the chimney piece of the great hall. In its last years it was tenanted by a local farmer. When Bowaters Paper Mills wished to extend their mills in the 1930s, it was demolished.

Poole Hall.

Stoak Village.

Stoak and Stanney

Though in fact they are a few miles apart, Stoak and Stanney are always spoken of collectively. There is an old three line verse, "In Stoak thereby few gradely folk, in Stanney hardly any, except John Grace and Nanny".

The parish church of St. Lawrence is a very ancient church, restored in 1827. It contains the vaults of the Bunbury family, and rare funeral hatchments belonging to them. Here too are the private pews of the Grace family of Whitby Hall. Alongside the canal this church was popular with boat families of Ellesmere Port. The local inn, the "Bunbury Arms", has been in existence for many, many years. But the nearest shop has always been in Little Stanney.

Here over fifty years ago the general store was run by a family called Burrels. Also here was the local smithy, and the blacksmith was a Mr. Warmington. In the timber yard adjoining the smithy was a hut for the local postman's use. Nearby Carter's farm was noted for its cheesemaking, and every Sunday evening a Chapel service was held for local inhabitants in the building where the cheese was made.

There has been a water mill at Stanney since 1546–47, till it ceased working just before the First World War. The last miller was a Mr. Dodd. If one was sent to the baker's in town for bread it was sold by weight, a slice being added if the loaf was under weight, and usually consumed on the way back. The Sunday School children on their outing to Frodsham Hill, would be taken in milk floats to Ellesmere Port Station, and at the end of the day the train would be met and they would be brought back to the villages the same way.

Capenhurst

Capenhurst is mentioned in the Domesday Book as Capeles. It also had its own local aristocratic family of the same name, who resided here from the 13th to the 16th century. The view shows it in the early 1900s. Today the ultra-modern atomic energy factory dominates the landscape. But in the village is evidence of an institution which was old when the Normans first came – a pound or pinfold. Domestic animals were impounded for debt and left there under the care of the public pound keeper, at the owner's expense. The keeper was obliged to retain all animals brought to him, but the owner had the right of rescue as they were being driven there by the aggrieved person. The pinfold belonged to the town or village, and was also used for the retention of any animal found straying on the public highway. This and the one at Spital, are the only ones left in Wirral.

Great Sutton *(right)*

"The White Swan" has had slight changes of name in its history. In 1851 it was known as the "Swan Inn" and kept by a Mr. Robert Platt. In 1869 it was called the "Black Swan" and kept by a Mr. Thomas E. Peers.

The Manor *(below left)*

When it was first erected this building was of modest proportions and was called "The Elms". It gradually became extended when a family called Owens were in residence, and became known as "Great Sutt-on-Manor". In those days, apart from schoolrooms there were no village halls, so some of the gentry would give a servants' ball for their staff, and the Owens from the Manor ran theirs on a grand scale. It was a non-stop do from 8 o'clock in the evening until it was time to go to work next morning.

Great Sutton Church *(below right)*

Although part of the Parish of Eastham, for many years church services were held in the shippon of Church Farm. This church of "St. John the Evangelist" was not opened until 1880. It had no organ for 27 years until 1927, when a bazaar was held and enough money raised to buy one.

Great Sutton.

The Manor Great Sutton

E SUTTON.

Little Sutton

The first picture shows a fish and vegetable shop that belonged to a Mr. T. Jones, a Primitive Methodist Chapel, and in the distance can be seen Ledsham Road corner.

The second view taken at Ledsham Road corner, shows Lockett's Bakehouse and Corn Factor. The gardens of the houses on the opposite side have all been converted into the shops.

The third view is looking towards the Old Red Lion.

Behind the group of people was Walker's Chemist shop, in a corner of which was the local Post Office. A local resident recalled when he was a telegraph boy in 1918, the assistant in the shop would knock on the window when he was required.

OLDE RED LION HOTEL, LITTLE SUTTON.

Little Sutton National School
(Red Lion Inn Club Room)

The first National School was held in the old Red Lion Inn Club Room. The licensee at this time was a Mrs. Tyrell, and a Mr. Burt was the schoolmaster. Frequent visitors were Canon Eaton who invariably wore a large Scotch plaid around his shoulders; the curate named Bourne, who came from Eastham; Mrs. Naylor from Hooton Hall, her two daughters Mitty and Mary, who were aged about six or seven, and who were usually attired in long red cloaks; Mr. Thorne, father of Mrs. Naylor, who made teaching the first class boys his hobby.

Of all of the days of the year, not even excepting Christmas Day, Chester Race Day was the greatest event for the boys of this school. In the days before motors were even dreamt of, everybody went by horse-drawn vehicles or else 'shanks' pony'. On this day hundreds of men, women and children, walked many miles to Chester Races. Very early in the morning, even before dawn, the main Birkenhead to Chester Road would be thronged with people. All the traffic from Liverpool, Birkenhead and the surrounding districts came through Little Sutton. Hundreds of carriages and horse-drawn vehicles of all kinds came through the village, invariably stopping at the Red Lion for refreshment. When starting off the boys used to call out to them: "Time, time, Chester Race time –
Cracking nuts and drinking wine",
and run after the carriages. Some would throw coppers and some would put them on the carriage steps, and woe unto the boy who essayed to remove the coppers from the steps. His hat would be fished off with a stick, and it would be carried half a mile or more before it was returned, the boy having to run after the carriage to recover it. The cap, however, was never returned without a generous contribution of coppers being placed inside. Some of the more agile boys could make as much as four or five shillings in this way on Chester Race Day.

STATION RD →

Hooton Hall and Parish Church

Hooton Parish Church is, in fact, in the village of Little Sutton, close to the main entrance of the old hall, where the lodge gates still stand. In 1847 the Hooton estate was sold to a Mr. R. C. Naylor. The church was erected in 1858 as a tribute to his first wife Mary Sophia. She unfortunately died giving birth to her child, who also died.

The top photograph shows on the left Old Berwick Road School. On the right, Basnett's had a shoe shop, and made boots for the local railway men. Other shops were Bowyer's the butchers; Williams, the dairy; Twaites, and Flacketts.

The lower view shows Station Road. The first building was a Private School with a Mr. Turner for the headmaster, later a branch Library, now used by The British Red Cross. The next building was the Police Station. Across the main road was the old Railway Hotel.

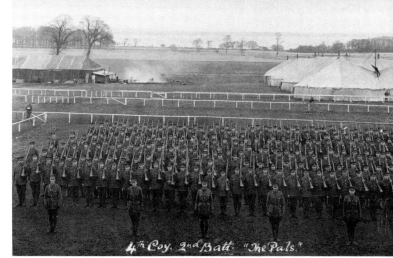

4th Coy, 2nd Batt. "The Pals."

Hooton Hall

The "Hooton Hall" illustrated, was the second one to be built here, the first one was demolished in 1778. Here the aristocratic Stanley family lived for over 500 years. Because of gambling debts the estate had to be sold. Mr. Naylor spent over £50,000 on the hall. His second wife's health broke down so he went to live at his Northamptonshire seat. The authorities wanted to increase his rates, and this so annoyed him that he removed all his furniture and the hall lay empty paying no rates.

During the First World War, it was used as a convalescent home for the overseas sick or wounded, as the picture shows. In the grounds tents were erected, and various military units received training. In the Church Parade view can be seen the grandstand of the old race course. The 2nd Batt. "The Pals", shown in the other picture, were not sent to the Western Front, they went to India. When America came into the war, the old racecourse was turned into an airfield to train American airmen.

In 1930 Henry Ford's American Works sent two passenger planes in crates, conveyed by the ship "Bellflower" to Ellesmere Port. They arrived at the New Jetty on Friday 17th of October, then were conveyed to Hooton Airfield, assembled and tested on the Saturday. By 1931 a firm named Comper Swift Aircraft Co. Ltd. were manufacturing their own local aircraft. It was called the "Swift", 50h.p. Salmoned-engined, with a cruising speed of 100m.p.h. and a climb of 600ft. per minute.

At the same time there was a thriving flying club.

Sadly at the same period Hooton Hall was bought by the Hooton Hall Development Co. and they demolished the old building.

Childer Thornton

This area has been recorded on land deeds going back
centuries. Astride the main turnpike from Chester to
Birkenhead it became a refreshment stop when in 1774
the first stage coach began to run from Chester to New
Ferry. At that time the public house was called the
"Fox and Hounds"; later on this was replaced by the
"Rifleman's Arms", and about 1893 the "Halfway
House" was built. A stone signpost not far away erected
by the Cheshire County Council in 1896, reads 8 miles
to Chester, 7¼ miles to Birkenhead, 1½ miles to
Eastham. Thus Childer Thornton was seen to be
halfway between Chester and Birkenhead hence the
name of the public house. The first view shows the
village from the Chester direction, the second from
Birkenhead. A little further on towards Birkenhead,
Hooton Corner was often the scene of a hectic sporting
event. In this instance a cross country run. Near here
was situated "Hooton Gate", one of the turnpike gates.

Eastham Church and Village

Until the 1860s, with the exception of part of Whitby which was in the Parish of Stoak, the remainder of the villages were in the Parish of Eastham. Within the parish church of St. Mary is the Stanley Chapel where many generations of the Stanley family lie buried in the vault below. The vault of the Pooles, believed to be extensive, lies near the altar rails in the chancel. In the graveyard, inscribed on the tombstones are the names of the Whitby, Sutton and Hooton families.

FRY'S CHOCOLATE

HOOTON
ARMS.

POST OFFICE